MW00943129

Rosey the Nosy Deer:
A TRUE STORY

The Wonderful Deer who Blessed the Residents of
Redbird Road for More than 21 Years

by Martha Knight

Xulon PRESS

1 John 5: 14-15, NIV

This is the confidence we have in approaching God; that if we ask anything according to His will, He hears us. And if we know He hears us – whatever we ask – we know that we have what we ask of Him.

1 Corinthians 13:13

And now these three remain: faith, hope, and love. But the greatest of these is love.

A tiny thing, no higher than my knee and not afraid of anything (sketch by author)

Dedication

This book is dedicated to A. W. Tieken – Grandpa (1931-1995). He was an extraordinary man, friend, and companion. He had so much enthusiasm for life, and together we not only helped raise Rosey but also game birds, Emus, goats, chickens, guineas, and our donkey Nudger. Grandpa was the spark that got this book started, way back in 1989.

Acknowledgements

There are so many people to thank that I am afraid the acknowledgements may be longer than the book. Grandpa started the project as a story to tell our grandchildren, but then Rosey outlived him by 10 years. The story became mine to tell.

Thank you to my many neighbors, all of whom were very helpful in sharing memories about "their" deer. They include Bruce and Judy Maxwell, Tim Elder and Gail Wilson, Ross and Darlene Astuto, Ken and Gloria Blackstone, Jesse and Velia Valdez, Mike and Michelle Matthews, Henry Young, Jimmy and Marsha Russell, the Deasons, and the Israels.

Thanks also to Tieken's children: Richard, Mark, Karen, and Brenda and their families; and to my children: Kerri and Kip and their families, and Tamera – who as a real estate broker found our special "heaven on earth" playground – and her family.

I also would like to thank Dr. Lois Parker, who first edited the manuscript in 1990; Drs. J.J. and Sharon Johnson, who also edited; and Dr. Eric Hazell, the final editor; the charter members of the San Gabriel Writers' League in Georgetown, Texas, including the writing group of Vivian Kirkbride, along with Dede Harper and Joy Lewis Nord.

Most of all, I thank God and give Him the glory for bringing such a wonderful blessing into our lives for so long. Rosey provided companionship and love for ten years after Grandpa died – God knew just what I needed in order to keep living, loving, and laughing. Together, God, Rosey, and my wonderful blended family carried me through deaths, financial difficulties, and many health issues.

Over time, the cabin and Rosey's presence became a place of peace and calm for friends and family. The grandkids always wanted to stay with us as long as possible in the summers. And I will never forget the day a friend called me at work and asked, "Can I just go sit on your front porch by myself for a while to commune with nature?" We both knew that "by myself" meant her and Rosey.

Of course, I must thank Rosey as well. She was the miracle who inspired this book.

Table of Contents

Chapter 1   We Meet Rosey 11

Chapter 2   Getting a Deer Education 23

Chapter 3   Rosey's Smorgasbord 35

Chapter 4   Rosey the Athlete 43

Chapter 5   Close Calls and other Mysteries 51

Chapter 6   Friends, Foes, and Food 63

Chapter 7   The "Teenage" Years. 69

Chapter 8   Rosey Finds a Friend 75

Chapter 9   Rosey – and Sometimes I – Raise a Family 83

Chapter 10 Strong to the End 95

Chapter 11 Our Teacher, or "The Gospel According

to Rosey". 103

Chapter 1

We Meet Rosey

You might not believe that a single white-tailed deer could change an entire neighborhood.

But Rosey was not your typical deer.

That's what I realized one day in 2005 as I stood clicking photographs of her: This marvelous old doe, blind in one eye, with crippling arthritis and a droopy ear, had been with us for more than two decades.

Most deer live in the wild for only seven to twelve years, but as I said, Rosey was not your typical deer.

It wasn't just her long life span that blessed the residents of Redbird Road for all that time. It was her status as a member of our community. In fact, just about every snapshot taken in this old country neighborhood from 1984 to 2005 contains that nosy little doe somewhere in the picture.

Once, she even called on me to help deliver her babies! Not long after that, I spotted a small herd of does browsing calmly in the woods, some of them heavy with fawns. I knew they were all her offspring.

They felt like my family, too.

Oh the stories we lived, the cherished memories, and the things she taught us. Our children grew from teens to adults to parents, and our grandchildren grew to adulthood, all within Rosey's lifetime.

Perhaps we should have named her "Miracle," because that is exactly what she turned out to be.

****

Let me go back to the beginning. This story of love and hope, of life and death struggle, started in the summer of 1984.

It started with some howling coyotes and a bag of Fritos.

We lived in Georgetown, Texas, 30 miles north of Austin. We wanted some land west of town, in the beautiful Texas hill country, with its trees, rocks, brush, and animals, all spread out over rolling, rugged hills. However, our daughter, a real estate broker, insisted on taking us to one of her listings *east* of town, which is farmland. Imagine our surprise when the acreage turned out to be solid trees and brush – it was an outcropping of the hill country. It had just enough pasture to raise a few goats, chickens, and even a cow or horse. Delighted, we purchased it.

Right away, we identified all kinds of native birds and wild animals on the property. Looking up, we saw cardinals, chickadees, hummingbirds, quail, wren, bluebirds, painted buntings, orioles, owls, and hawks. Looking around, we noticed raccoons, armadillos, opossums, squirrels, coyotes, fox, skunks, and even bobcats.

To our surprise, though, we saw no deer, even after several weeks. Disappointed but thankful for the beautiful land, we started clearing a road and some space for a small cabin. I loved it so much I stated, "With a few deer this would be heaven on earth."

Well, "Ask and you shall receive."

One sunny afternoon in June that year, Grandpa and I with two of our grandchildren, Sara and Clay, drove out to our still-new acreage to clear land and plant some roses. After a few hours of wrestling with brush and briars, we rested and ate our picnic lunch.

I saw something moving in the brush and whispered, "Shhh! Look over there." An animal emerged into a clearing. A tiny thing, it stood no higher than my knee, with four little toothpick legs. Small white spots sprinkled its golden brown hair. Its short tail was brown on top and white on the bottom, and very big ears outlined its face. We stared in awe.

Sara whispered, "Is it a little lamb?"

There are in fact sheep in the area, and one may have drifted away from the herd. But this animal's hair was straight, and its tail shorter than a sheep's.

"Is it a goat?" she asked.

I looked at the ears. Goats' ears are floppy, but this animal's ears stood straight up and twitched. Oh! I could see a healed-over cut in the left ear, part of which was missing. Because I could see the cut even at this distance, I knew it had been a severe injury, and it would mark this animal for the rest of its life.

Sara grew more impatient. "What is it Grandma? Is it a deer?"

It walked closer and turned sideways. That was when I knew for sure. A male has swirls on its head where antlers will grow. "Yes," I answered her. "It's a little fawn, a female deer. A doe."

Now it was Clay's turn. "Is she lost? Where are her mama and daddy? Why isn't she scared? Is she hungry?"

Grandpa and I answered these questions as best we could, and while we did, the little deer walked toward us. Deer usually keep their distance from people, but this one strolled right up, her big brown eyes investigating us as we investigated her.

"Can I pet her?" Clay wondered aloud.

If we touched her she might run, and her mama might smell human hands and never let the baby nurse again. It was not worth the risk.

I answered, "I'm afraid not. She belongs in the woods and her mother may be looking for her. She must be free to do whatever she wants."

I added, "Deer are wild animals."

But then, that little deer lifted her nose and started smelling our food. "She must be hungry," Sara said.

"When they are hungry, wild animals come close to humans," Grandpa agreed.

I myself knew a little about what fawns needed. I grew up watching wild deer and felt they were almost magical. When my dad and brothers hunted them, I "hunted" with my camera, taking more pictures than I could count. Also, just a few years before this day, I had taken a wildlife rescue class.

Deer eat leaves, weeds, grain, and vegetables. While leaves and weeds grew where this little doe could reach, I didn't know if she was old enough to eat them. And unfortunately, we did not have any vegetables that day.

But we did have Fritos.

Deer certainly eat corn, and we had brought some Fritos corn chips to go with our sandwiches.

We stood, amazed and silent, as that fawn walked right up to a very surprised Clay and smelled his chips. "Hold one out for her and see what happens," I suggested. She sniffed but didn't eat. Clay dropped the chips to the ground.

The doe sniffed at them again. This time she tried one. We all giggled as she snapped up those chips one at a time with her tongue and shoved them into her mouth. Crunch, crunch, crunch, and they were gone.

We tossed more chips. She sniffed, ate one, and walked away. "Maybe she's looking for her mother," Clay said.

A short distance away, the doe started eating leaves from the young sprouts of a native persimmon tree. She chewed a mouthful and then – she came back for more corn chips!

I suppose most of us like a few bites of this and a few bites of that at our meals, and apparently, this doe did too.

We meet Rosey. Part of her left ear was missing.

Deer do not need to chew their food the way we do, because they have four stomachs. They swallow fast at first, and they belch it up and chew later when they are in a safe place away from varmints or predators. We watched this one grab the end pieces of the bush, which is the newest growth, and chew and swallow.

Deer also have front and back teeth. The back teeth are on both the bottom and top jaw, but the front teeth are on the bottom only. Cattle, moose, buffalo, and elk have the same kind of teeth and eat the same way. Instead of teeth on top in front, they have a rough, strong gum or pad. This helps them hold the leaves that they bite off branches.

After sharing our food, we decided the neighborly thing would be to offer this deer something to drink. We had a jug of water and Sara found a dog dish in the car. When she put the bowl on the ground, the deer just casually strolled over, eating some leaves here and there on the way. She smelled the water and turned around. We decided she wasn't thirsty but instead just wanted to investigate the bowl.

And wouldn't you know it: next, she decided to investigate us. She walked over and smelled our clothes and our shoes. "You sure are nosy, little deer." Clay laughed.

I fetched my camera from the car and cautiously began snapping pictures, using a whole roll of film. I marveled that the deer was not disturbed by the camera, by our quick movements, or simply by our talking. She stayed calm as could be and did what she wanted.

Soon, the sun began setting as a beautiful full moon rose, shimmering through the trees. We needed to head home.

Suddenly, we heard coyotes howling on the big ranch east of us. The evening stillness carried their shrieks a great distance, making their high-pitched relay message seem very close. And very eerie.

Sara shuddered. "Grandpa, will her mother find her?"

We had seen no other deer at any time out here, so we didn't know where this one came from, who she left, or who might have abandoned her.

Sara and Clay asked the question that Grandpa and I both anticipated: "Can we take her with us? Please?"

Grandpa looked at me, shook his head, and answered, "No, I'm sorry kids, but it is against the law to move a deer if it's healthy. She seems to be plenty healthy. She may belong to someone. She has to stay here. Her mother may be watching us from the bushes right now."

The coyotes howled again.

Grandpa looked at the kids and said, "We can pour out the rest of the chips, the bread and everything else in the car that is edible. We can leave the bowl of water and come back to check on her tomorrow."

We walked back to the car, climbed in to leave, and turned to wave goodbye.

Guess what?

Our nosy little deer marched right up and started smelling inside the car. Then she walked over to the roses we had just planted and started nibbling.

"Oh dear, I hope she doesn't destroy them," I declared. "Tell her good-bye and let's try to think of a good name for her before we come back."

"Will she really be here when we come back?" Clay asked. "I think we made a friend. She didn't seem afraid at all."

Grandpa and I couldn't help it. We lingered, reluctant to leave the magic we had discovered. Finally, though, we drove away, each of us feeling sad on the way back to town. All the way, Sara and Clay peppered us with more questions about the nosy little deer that walked into our lives.

"Let's get out the encyclopedia as soon as we get home and study about our nosy little deer," Sara said.

"*Our* deer," I asked? "The one eating my roses?"

"That's it!" Clay exclaimed. "She nibbled your rose bushes, Grandma, and like Sara said, she's nosy. So let's name her Rosey the nosy deer."

We all agreed immediately.

What a fabulous journey we had begun.

Chapter 2

Getting a Deer Education

A mong the many unexpected pleasures Rosey gave us over the years, one of the first was an education about deer.

That evening after our adventure on our new land, Sara came to the dinner table carrying the *World Book Encyclopedia*. Remember, this was 1984, long before the Internet. "Look, Clay," she said. "Rosey is a white-tailed deer, an **Odocoileus Virgianianus**." She pronounced each syllable carefully. "Texas has more white-tailed deer than any other region in the world. Since the bears and panthers went away, there are *too* many deer in some areas."

"Why did the bears and panthers go away?" Clay wondered.

Grandpa answered, "Well, their habitat didn't really go away. The country is still perfect for them and there are still a few around, but most of them have been killed off because people are scared of them."

"Do they get their name just from the little white spot we saw?" Clay continued to question.

I knew a little about deer, but I had to borrow the encyclopedia from Sara to make sure I answered correctly. I said, "The basic color is brown, with the tail brown on the outside and white underneath. The white is usually hidden because the tail hangs down, but when deer get scared or angry their tail goes straight up and spreads out. The white part can be seen that way, and it acts as an alert to other deer."

"Like a flag," Clay said.

"Exactly."

We read that deer have the big scientific name of *Chordata Vertebrata Mammalia Ungulata*. <u>Chordata</u> means that it has a backbone like humans. <u>Vertebrata</u> means it has a brain inside a skull, and the brain is connected to the backbone. It also means that the backbone is segmented into parts that move. <u>Mammalia</u> means that it is a mammal, a warm-blooded animal. <u>Ungulata</u> means that is has hooves on its legs instead of claws or nails.

"Rosey has hooves on her feet that are split into two parts. Kind of like two large finger nails," Clay remembered.

"Yes," I agreed. "And cows, goats, sheep, elk, and moose also have split hooves."

"Are humans mammals?" he continued.

"We certainly are. We are like deer in many ways. Fortunately, though, we have fingernails instead of hooves."

"If you ask me, they're just deer," Grandpa smiled. "Enough of all this science."

Grandpa's "deer education" came more from observation than from books

As Grandpa and I expected, the kids woke up the next morning anxious to head back out to the property. They had only one more day to visit, and they begged us to let them spend it in the country. As soon as they gobbled down their breakfast, we drove out to see if "our" deer was still there. This time we took shelled corn, more corn chips, and sunflower seeds.

We drove up to our destination, and all of us – even Grandpa – craned our necks in every direction. We saw no deer. My roses had been nibbled but were still standing. Some of the water was gone but not all of it.

The kids bombarded us with questions.

"Did the deer drink it?"

"Could be."

"Or was it rabbits?"

"That's possible."

"Or was it birds, or some other animal?"

"All animals need water," Grandpa answered. "Deer can get moisture and water from plants; plus, creeks and ponds provide water for all wild animals," he added.

"We have a pond here, right? Sara asked

"That's right, and a creek runs through the land right next to ours."

We waited for what seemed like hours, quietly exploring the wild beauty around us. Finally, we got our tools and started clearing brush, talking, and just generally making plenty of racket.

And out of the bushes walked Rosey.

We knew it was her because we saw the same little cut on her left ear. No disaster befell her during the night, and now we were glad we left her in the woods.

We studied the white spots on her back, her overall size, and the length of her legs. Based on what Grandpa and I knew about deer, plus what we had read in the encyclopedia, we estimated that she was about two months old. She was a fawn and would be called a fawn until she was a year old. Then she would be called a yearling.

Well, she was even less shy than the day before. She came right up and sniffed us again, exploring at her leisure.

But all of a sudden she froze, raised her head, perked up her ears, and twitched them back and forth. It seemed that her ears moved constantly. We froze too and listened intently, but heard nothing.

She pointed her ears forward and sure enough, we heard a rustle of leaves under the thick brush. We stared with great anticipation, and soon we saw – a little cottontail rabbit.

Before we could even start laughing though, we heard the thin, fierce shriek of a red-tailed hawk. We looked back and forth, up to the sky and down to the ground. As the hawk passed over, the little rabbit froze, and then it hurried back under the cover of the thick brush. The hawk spun lazily along, and once again, we fielded questions from the kids.

"What was that?" Did the rabbit know the hawk was there? Was the rabbit scared of it, or us?"

When we answered these questions, our attention came back to Rosey. Sara wondered out loud, "What did she look like when she was born? Was she helpless? Did her mom care for her? Do deer get sick when it rains or when it gets real cold?"

I sure felt grateful for my wildlife rescue class and the encyclopedia. I told her, "Fawns are usually born from April to June. Newborns seem shaky, like they can't get around, but they sure can. Not long after they are born, they can keep up with their mothers. The mothers are very protective and keep fawns in the tall grass and brush. The mothers leave to find food while the babies stay in that safe area. While lying there, a fawn won't move much unless it is disturbed."

A person who happens upon a white-tailed fawn curled up in a hiding place might think it is alone and helpless. People are often tempted to pet those cute little things or even adopt them as pets. But the mother is probably close by and will soon be back to let the fawn nurse. That's why it's best to observe awhile and move quietly away without handling or disturbing the animal.

Everyone offered guesses about what happened to Rosey's mother and how Rosey came to be here. Maybe her mother died. Maybe somebody found Rosey bedded down, thought she was helpless, and for some reason carried her over to this area. Maybe she got caught in a fence and someone saved her. That could be the reason for the cut on her ear.

Whatever had happened, she was here now, and we wanted to help her any way we could. The first thing we decided was to let her choose when and where she wanted to run and where she wanted to sleep. She should remain as wild and as free as she wanted.

Sara and Clay insisted that we spend all of their last day in the country. We identified the trees we wanted to protect: live oaks, redbuds, Mexican plums, Texas persimmon, and yaupon holly. We cleared out everything we didn't want: briars, cactus, and scrub bushes.

Rosey spent the entire day right by our sides.

She let us touch her with no problem. She ate some of the corn and just gobbled down the sunflower seeds. Occasionally she lay down, chewed her cud (I'll explain that later), watched us, and just hung out.

Eventually, the full moon appeared again, orange in the early evening light, then shining through the trees, and then becoming a buttery yellow as the night cleared. Sara and Clay both wanted to stay but were also anxious to go home and tell their parents and the kids at school about their great adventure and new friend.

They also felt confident that Rosey would be here when they returned.

****

After the grandkids went back home, Grandpa and I continued to come out to the property. Later that week we brought our dog Preacher with us. A border collie cross, he was black with a white "collar" of hair around his neck, and that's why, Grandpa said, we should name him Preacher. I liked to tease him and say, "No, you named him that so you could yell, 'Preacher! Hush!'"

Grandpa held him tight on a leash, and wouldn't you know, here came Rosey, nosing around. She didn't know what to think about the dog, and Preacher had never seen a deer.

When Preacher moved toward her, Rosey exploded. She ran through bushes and around trees, over some more bushes, and right back to where she started. Apparently, she wanted another look.

Very carefully and slowly, Preacher and Rosey smelled each other, and before long they had accepted each other as friends. Rosey could run faster, so we released Preacher and watched them cavort and chase each other all around until they wore themselves out – just like two children.

Grandpa and Preacher

Each weekend we came back. We continued to clear brush and we drew up plans for our small cabin back in the thickest woods, a place to stay until we had time to build a bigger house closer to the road. We saw other houses in the area, usually spaced about two or three city blocks apart, with no close neighbors like there are in town. Also, our friends and family learned about Rosey and visited often.

Every time we came, Rosey showed up, just like it was her territory too.

I considered it typical white-tailed deer country, past all the farms and crops, on a hillside covered with trees. Female deer have a territory of about one mile from their birthplace, while males travel a little farther out.

Our neighbors were in Rosey's territory too. Grandpa and I often walked on the chalky white, limestone-gravel road, periodically meeting and visiting with them. The road dead-ends about a mile down, with trees on both sides and thick brush underneath. Our acreage is about a half mile north of the paved county road, and the road continues north for about another half mile.

The road was in horrible condition, and the neighbors at the back end often bogged down in the mud when it rained. A few times they

32

had to call a tow truck. Now, when the rains made it muddy, they would park their car close to our driveway and walk home.

As we talked to them and our other neighbors, we were amazed at what we discovered.

Chapter 3

Rosey's Smorgasbord

O f the many blessings Rosey brought to our lives, one was that she helped make our neighborhood a kind of big, extended family. This began to happen when we discovered that we weren't the only ones in the area who knew Rosey. In fact, the entire neighborhood had "adopted" her. She belonged to all of us, and she gave us all something in common.

Altogether, twenty families own land on our road, but only nine houses existed back in Rosey's early years. We all visited, either on walks or when people driving home would stop and chat with someone working in a yard. First, we met the Maxwells, who were walking along the road with a little boy strapped on his Dad's back.

We chatted for a while and eventually asked, "Have you seen a little fawn out here about knee high?"

"We are pretty sure there are no deer out here, except our little one we named Baby."

Grandpa and I immediately knew what that meant.

Well, the Blackstones, who lived across from us and were clearing land for a home, claimed "Daisy" as their own. So did the Elders, who also called her Daisy. Mr. Young, a Chippewa Indian who lived at the end of the road, called her "Bidaban," a Chippewa name meaning doe fawn. The Russels, across from Mr. Young, named her "Flag." Apparently, she also answered to Marcie, Bonnie, Bambi, Deerie, Nancy, Susie, Cactus, Honey, Emma, Shirley – and even Deer Abby.

When Mr. King, an old time rancher in the area, said Rosey was the only deer he had seen in this part of the country in many years, we knew for sure we had something special.

The view from the cabin toward Redbird Road

And sure enough, Rosey became the "star" of the whole neighborhood. She enjoyed what surely was the best and most varied diet of us all. In addition to our corn and sunflower seeds, she grazed at one neighbor's cow trough. She ate dog food at the house with five dogs. She took her share from the Elders' prized vegetable garden. She munched on crackers, chips, raw potatoes, carrots, corn meal, and watermelon rind. This came in addition to the leaves, grass, brush, berries, acorns, and fruit she picked from in the wild.

Grown deer eat about ten pounds of green stuff a day, and we guessed she must have eaten all that plus everyone's goodies. She even got picky. She would not eat any meat, and although she loved all kinds of chips, she turned up her nose at pork rind chips.

37

When we tilled up land for a garden, it quickly became her favorite spot, right in the middle. She loved any type of flower, whether it was from gardens, weeds, or brush.

But her favorite was roses. How she loved roses! We built a fence around our rose and vegetable garden, and the Blackstones built a greenhouse. They grew a rare variety called OJ roses, which are the color of orange juice. Gloria said, "They must be as sweet as orange juice too, because Rosey goes for them every chance she gets."

Other neighbors had fruit trees, and whenever Rosey saw a peach or a plum on the ground, she started eating. She would nibble for a moment and then – swoosh! – the whole thing would disappear into her mouth. She would chew and chew the pulp, and suddenly the seed would pop up out of the side of her mouth, all cleaned off and ready to grow. Seeds need only a little dirt on top and some rain, so just imagine how many seeds deer plant every year.

Rosey liked potato chips so much we decided she needed some salt. We put a little dab down in a pile. She sniffed but wouldn't eat it or lick it, so we bought a salt block from the feed store, which she did chew and lick occasionally.

It's kind of like the old infomericals say – but wait, there's more! The diet of deer also includes some dry brown plants, dead leaves, and weeds. Rosey ate dry leaves off the ground and off the trees in the winter. She ate thorny thistles after they died and dried. Apparently, deer need some dry food, just as horses need hay. Or maybe Rosey just needed it to manage the neighborhood smorgasbord swirling around in her digestive system.

She loved anything made from flour. She ate bread, rolls, biscuits, and cookies, and would always choose bread products over corn or maize. We bought day old or expired bread for her, but she didn't care. She ate it all.

With my wildlife rescue class, the encyclopedia, and especially just observation, we all received a remarkable education about deer. For example, we thought Rosey ate grass, but when we watched closely, we noticed that she ate only the weeds growing in between the various grasses. Also, acorns are often the primary food for wild deer. They eat these from oak trees in the fall, and often, their physical condition depends on the supply of acorns.

The biggest surprise, though, had to be the jellybeans.

Our grandchildren, Sara and Clay, once brought a sack of jelly-beans to test on Rosey. The kids held out fistfuls of the little candies, and we all stared in wonder as Rosey's tongue darted out and snatched one – then another, and another, and another. She ate the entire sack, one jellybean at a time. She probably wondered if they grew on some kind of magical berry tree.

When the Russells later told us she loved Skittles, we weren't surprised at all.

Grandma – that's me – petting Rosey

When deer are full, they rest and chew their cuds. Now this is a sight to see. In the throat area, a lump of food comes up from the first stomach, back into the mouth. You can actually see it travel up from the first stomach, along the long neck and back into the mouth. It is a moving bump, about the size of a lemon. Next, it is belched up.

It takes them about three minutes to chew an average of 40 times. They swallow it again, and down it goes into stomach number two, to be digested some more. You can see it go back down, just like you see it on the way up. In a few seconds, up comes another lump. This happens over and over until the first stomach is about empty.

There are poison plants in the area, and Rosey, being so nosy, had to try them. Once she tasted just a small bit of a "Death Camas" plant. We could tell she did not like it because her tongue started working back and forth on her lips. She snorted a couple times, shook her head back and forth, twitched her ears, shook her head again, and spit it back out!

If we spoke deer language, we would have warned her. We tried to warn her anyway, but it didn't work. And with no mother or other deer to teach her, she had to learn for herself, with only her instincts to guide her. I like to call those instincts her "memories."

One day Rosey decided to try mistletoe. Mistletoe is a poisonous parasite plant that grows wild on trees. It's the same plant people use on Christmas and New Year as decorations. Both the plant and berries are poison to people, but apparently not to Rosey. She nibbled on a few leaves, then on the berries. She stopped and walked away, but turned around and went back for more.

There seemed to be no end to Rosey's eating adventures, especially considering that one day I thought I was going to have to try the Heimlich maneuver on her. We were clearing brush, and filling bird feeders with seed and hummingbird feeders with sugar water. I didn't see Rosey but threw several slices of bread on the ground for later.

Right away, here she came running. She looked hungry, and she grabbed, gobbled, and swallowed one slice of bread, and another, and another.

Then it happened! She swallowed too much food too quickly. It hung in her throat. We could see the lump. Rosey was choking right before our eyes.

She raised her front feet. She swung her head around, jumped on her hind feet, and back on the ground. She tried to cough. No luck. We watched helplessly. She darted around, knocking over some flowerpots and prancing like a horse.

This is when we decided to try the Heimlich. Unfortunately, however, we couldn't catch her.

Finally, the knot in her throat started back toward her mouth instead of her stomach. She spit it out on the ground and was normal almost right away. She went right back to the bread, but she ate much more slowly this time.

Lesson learned.

Chapter 4

Rosey the Athlete

*A*ll of us on "Redbird Road" did everything we could to keep Rosey around. Although she was a free soul, we all called her "our deer." She even helped us welcome visitors, approaching them and smelling, and letting just about anyone pet, feed, and even hug her. Soon, all of us in the neighborhood had to choose: either let Rosey eat whatever she wanted, or build a high fence around the plants we didn't want her to eat. I can tell you, our neighborhood ended up with a lot of high fences.

We called our road Redbird Road because of the many beautiful cardinals in the area. The county would not help grade or pave it until at least 80% of the lots had homes on them, so Grandpa decided we should form a Road Association. We tracked down home addresses using courthouse records, wrote letters, met more of our neighbors, and eventually started our organization. Grandpa became the president. We collected money and hired a contractor to grade our road and add gravel.

This meant we could build our cabin and spend more time in the country, which in turn meant we could pal around with Rosey even more.

A few months had passed since her choking scare, and she continued to grow and change. The white spots on her back began to fade, still there, but more dull. The rusty, golden brown hair began to turn gray.

Rosey usually walked, ran, or stood still, but occasionally she would lie down. We watched her do it. While horses fold their back legs first, Rosey folded all four at once, until her stomach touched the ground. She held her head high. In this position, she usually chewed her cud or took naps. Sometimes she bent her head down and laid it on her front feet and legs in a sort of cuddle, but her eyes, ears, and nose were always working.

It is amazing to see just how vigilant and wary a deer can be. Every once in a while, Rosey fell into a deep sleep, with her head on the ground and resting on her chin, but most of the time she took short naps. For the entire time, she held her head high, her ears twitching for any sign of danger, her eyes only partially closed and then all the way open, then partially closed again. This half-asleep, half-awake napping showed us that she almost always stayed at an alert status.

When an "alarm" sounded – a rattling in the bushes, or any unfamiliar noise – Rosey's back feet and legs dug into the ground and pushed up. Like a jack-in-a-box, her front legs went out straight and she hit the ground six feet away, already running before you even noticed something had scared her.

In fact, as we discovered in yet another dramatic moment, a professional basketball player could only dream of jumping like Rosey. In the fall of 1984, we started building the cabin, which meant we needed a septic tank, because there is no city sewer system. We dug a hole, six feet by nine feet. The sides were straight down – seven feet. After we completed the first day of digging, sure enough here came Rosey to investigate. One minute she was sniffing and nosing around, and then, with no warning, she just jumped in. She didn't slip and fall. She jumped, on purpose. Seven feet down.

Now what? Unfortunately, my wildlife rescue class never covered "how to rescue a deer from a septic tank hole." The encyclopedia certainly wouldn't help either.

Rosey investigates the septic tank hole

We brainstormed a while. Pulling her out with a rope seemed the best way, but we had tried a little halter with her once before and discovered right away that she despised being tethered to a rope. Would we actually have to dig a trench on one side so she could walk out?

Meanwhile, Rosey, who stood about two and a half feet tall, seemed perfectly content seven feet down. Apparently, she thought we had built a new room, just for her. She smelled the dirt on the sides and below. She walked around, investigating every aspect of that hole.

Finally satisfied with her little exploration, Rosey moved to the edge of the wall. She looked up. She looked down. Then, she bent very slightly, and…whoosh – she jumped with all four feet at once, straight up and out of that hole!

Right at that moment, we knew that all those fences built in the neighborhood to keep her out were inadequate. In fact, they seemed almost like a game to her. Rather than even attempting to crawl through or scoot under, Rosey would just stand in front of our fence, which was six feet high. She would look left and right to make sure all was okay, and then, with no running start, she would sail right over the top.

Rosey could jump for accuracy as well as distance and height. One time our neighbor, Bruce Maxwell, decided to install a radio in his station wagon and asked another neighbor, Henry Young, to help. Both front car doors were open, with the radio in the front and the speakers in the back. Rosey the nosy deer checked it out, smelling everything. She loved a challenge.

With no warning, while Bruce and Henry both crouched to look up under the dash, Rosey jumped through the open doors, straight from one side of the car to the other. She never even touched the seat or the steering wheel – or Bruce or Henry either. When they felt the movement of air as she swooshed through, they both looked up in amazement and asked at the same time, "Did you see that?"

Rosey with Heather, the Maxwells' dog

If she preferred, Rosey could jump through small openings in a fence. Once, our neighbor Gail grew a garden that Rosey considered her very own. She visited and ate regularly, so Gail built a small fence with corner posts and chicken wire. Gail thought that two wires about a foot apart and four feet high would be enough.

Rosey strolled up, glanced at the space between the wires, and hopped right through. She must have considered the place a cafeteria, because she walked around, choosing first this plant and then that one.

Once it rained for several days straight, and shallow water stood everywhere. Quite a bit of water also collected in a small pond on the back part of our land. Grandpa and I had strolled over there, enjoying the scenery. We stood still in the calm breeze, the birds periodically chirping. It was very quiet.

Have you ever felt like you were being watched? We stood there a few minutes, and that's exactly what we felt. We turned from the water to go back to the cabin – and there stood Rosey. She sneaked up on us, coming from who knows where.

That was when we learned that deer can move almost silently.

She seemed ready to play. We knew her so well by now that we recognized the look in her eyes. Her head was swinging up and down as if she was nodding "yes."

Then she snorted!

The sound of a snort from a deer is difficult to describe. If you take a popped balloon and blow into the mouthpiece, you will have some idea of the raspy hiss sound that comes from a deer forcefully snorting air through its nose.

After she snorted, Rosey ran down to the pond, drank a little, and went deeper until she had all four feet in the water, just deep enough for splashing. Next, she raised her front feet and kicked, splashing water on her stomach. She reared up on her hind feet like a horse and jumped in completely. She ran from one side to the other, as fast as she could go, which was extremely fast. Water splashed everywhere.

She ran up on the banks of the pond, turned around, and came back through again.

Rosey goes for a swim

Every so often she would slam on her "brakes," digging all four feet into the mud. It seemed like an invitation for us to join her, but for now, we decided to let her have it all to herself.

She crossed the pond one more time, walked out, shook off, and faded into the brush and trees.

A good swimmer and an expert at the long jump and high jump, "our deer" had become quite the athlete.

Chapter 5

Close Calls and other Mysteries

"Untie that deer!" Grandpa shouted. "What do you think you're doing?"

The workers in the back of the truck looked at us and back at Rosey. Grandpa yelled again, "That's our deer!"

It was April 1985, and we had almost finished our cabin. We contracted for someone to build the shell, and Grandpa and I, along with our grown children, completed most of the work inside. Today, someone we hired was at the cabin blowing insulation into the ceiling, while we spent the day in town.

In the late afternoon Grandpa and I went out to see if the men had finished the job. Imagine our surprise when we drove up and saw Rosey tied in the back of their truck. She was fighting to get loose, jumping and kicking in desperation. We thought that surely she would hurt herself.

Grandpa leaped out of the car and started waving his hands and hollering at the workers. "No one messes with our deer!"

The workers immediately untied the deer and started explaining. "We thought it was wild. We wanted to show it to our kids."

Grandpa said, "I told your boss that we had a tame deer out here and that you could pet it and feed it, but it was not to be hurt or moved."

The workers left in a hurry. I said, "I think from now on we need to stay out here any time we hire help."

Grandpa agreed.

Our next scare happened six months later, when Rosey went missing. Actually, it was some time before we knew for sure she was missing, because deer change hair color to blend in with the environment.

Every fall, their hair changes from its summer reddish brown to a grayish black. Instead of a haircut, deer just shed old hair and replace it with new, kind of like putting on a coat. As the winter arrives, their hair becomes thicker, softer, shorter, and closer together. This "body wrap" protects them against the rain, snow, wind, and cold.

Deer can even control their hair. On cold or rainy days, they fluff it up all over their bodies. This keeps the cold out, and, almost like a tarpaulin, it just drains the rain off. It looks like a warm, cozy blanket wrapped around the whole body and even the legs. This also makes the animal look bigger.

Just imagine – so many different hair "styles" with no brush, blow dryer, or curling iron.

Because of all these changes, deer can be difficult to see, even when they are almost right in front of you. One day we saw Rosey step about two feet into the brush, but amidst all the brown leaves, gray tree trunks, and gray rocks, she just vanished. She could hide in almost any clump of bushes.

Sometimes we would look into the woods and see nothing but the green, brown, and gray of the trees and brush. We would look again, and there she was, as if she simply appeared from nowhere.

Even though Rosey could hide so well, she always made her regular appearances in the neighborhood. And so when no one saw her for a few days, we knew something had happened. Everyone kept a lookout. We began to think she had been hurt or even killed. All of us knew all along that this day might come, but now, faced with the possibility, we felt extremely sad.

We knew Rosey traveled mainly along the same trails. She seemed to create her own secret passageways in the trees and through the small openings. She also noticed everything. Her nose and ears moved constantly, and with the slightest change, she would stop dead still and wait until she figured things out. You could almost tell what she was thinking. Sometimes she would walk straight toward whatever animal or noise had interested her.

Rosey inspects the construction of our cabin

She mapped out her entire territory that way. If we cut down a tree, or even a single limb from a tree, she would know, and she would have to go smell the cut. When we planted a new bush or tree, drove a different car, or simply moved a plant from one side of the cabin to the other, she observed it and investigated.

Her nosiness always amused us, but had it gotten her in trouble now?

We all ventured our guesses and followed whatever seemed like a promising lead. We all walked around our properties and looked along some of Rosey's well-known travel routes. Any time any of us saw somebody in the area, we asked if they had seen her.

We heard stories about a deer seen in a cattle trailer over at the nearby country store. Was it her?

Coyotes were another possibility, and so were mountain lions. In fact, someone spotted a mountain lion on our road earlier that year. A county agent came out, examined the tracks, and confirmed that it was indeed a mountain lion. It roamed the area with two cubs, and usually stayed on some abandoned acreage near the back end of the road. The county agent said it was probably a female who stopped there to have babies. Hopefully, she moved on; mountain lions have a territory of about 100 miles.

I mentioned earlier that Rosey blessed us all by bringing the neighborhood together. She was like a family member that everybody shared in common.

Well, now we all shared the same fear for her.

One morning, three weeks after she disappeared, I glanced out in the yard – and there stood Rosey. You can imagine how thrilled Grandpa and I felt.

Right away, we noticed a big rope around her neck. It had been cut, broken, or chewed. We approached her, and while deer may not experience feelings the same way humans do, she sure looked happy to see us too. We cut the rope off her neck and doctored her abrasions. We felt very grateful to have our deer back.

Now, everyone in the neighborhood joined in celebrating. We all speculated about what had happened. Did those workers come back for her? If so, did someone come along and cut her loose? The rope was at least three quarters of an inch in diameter, about twice as big as a regular lariat. Breaking it or even chewing through it would have been extremely difficult.

We never solved the mystery, but everyone was happy to have her back.

While we never figured out what happened that time, we did solve the mystery of Rosey's origins. A neighbor behind Redbird Road on a big ranch had found her caught in a fence down in south Texas. He brought her up here, doctored her scratches and cuts, and bottle-fed her. That's how she became "imprinted" to humans. In this case, imprinting means the way an animal learns to respond to some type of touching or other action. When the rancher rescued her, Rosey learned to accept certain kinds of contact with humans.

The rancher also inserted a cattle tag in Rosey's ear, just as he did with his many cows. He said it took her about five minutes to tear it out.

Well, that explained the cut in her ear.

Two mysteries solved at once.

It turned out that Rosey didn't care for cattle, so when she got big enough to eat, she left. The rancher and his family thought something happened to her, and, just like all of us, they celebrated when they found out she was alive and thriving on Redbird Road.

Our finished cabin during a rare central Texas snow. Rosey always
found a way to get into every picture.

Another close call occurred with one neighbor who strongly
objected to Rosey's grazing in his garden. He called and asked the
wildlife department to remove her, but a game warden said that could
not be done legally. The warden suggested that a hunting license and
a gun might take care of the man's problem.

Fortunately, before that happened, word got around. Many of
the neighbors volunteered to help the man build a fence – a sturdy,
impassable, tall one – around his garden. He agreed and soon calmed
down. Eventually, he grew very fond of Rosey.

See what I mean about Rosey bringing us all together?

Over time, Rosey became something of an attraction. Many
people who did not live in the area heard about her and wanted to

drive out to pet and feed her. This became something of a common occurrence. It all worked out fine.

Except for once.

One cool, drizzly, foggy day, a friend visited with his two boys, who were six and four. Those boys wanted so badly to pet and feed Rosey, and they waited and waited until finally she stopped by. So much mud caked her hooves that it looked like she had put on socks. The boys went out and fed her, and began scratching her ears, throat, and back of her neck. Rosey loved that.

One of the boys began petting her back. Rosey liked to be scratched from the back of the neck downward, but, as we discovered, she did not care at all for the reverse. As the boy moved his fingers from her back toward her neck, Rosey's ears flattened.

Suddenly, she raised her front legs into the air and struck at the boy's back.

The legs of deer are extremely powerful. That's how Rosey could do a standing "high jump" straight out of our septic tank hole. In many instances, wild deer have injured people by rising up on the back legs and kicking with the front legs. Rosey's hooves could have really hurt that young boy.

Luckily, however, the mud on Rosey's feet, combined with the coat on the boy's back and the fact that she didn't kick him in the head, all worked together and there was no harm done. Of course it frightened the boy, who ran screaming to his dad. But the only physical damage was two streaks of mud down his coat.

We believed Rosey knew exactly what she was doing: sending a warning. After witnessing so many of her athletic feats, we knew that she could have easily kicked that boy in the head if she wanted to.

Rosey never tried that on a grownup, and she never did anything like that again, with anybody. We always petted her the right way afterwards, and we always closely supervised her "visitation" with children.

She may have been imprinted to humans, but Rosey still had the instincts of a wild animal.

"Our deer" experienced plenty of other scrapes and injuries. One day we noticed Rosey limping very badly. As we walked toward her we saw, to our shock, a badly mangled and bleeding right front leg. We could actually see down into the wound, all the way to the tendons and muscles. Thankfully, we didn't see any broken bones. Still, because of her pain, she wouldn't let us get close enough to examine her.

I called the neighbor across the road, who stayed home with her kids all day. She said she thought some dogs or coyotes had attacked Rosey. That was sure what it looked like, Grandpa and I agreed. The neighbor came over with some antibiotics and other medicine.

We all gathered around to see if we could doctor Rosey back to health.

She stood still for us as we approached her. We sprayed some of the medicine on her wound.

And she took off like a flash.

Time for Plan B. We thinned some iodine with water. Iodine can kill bacteria and other germs. Whenever we could get close enough, we would splash some of it on Rosey's wound before she would dart away again.

It was amazing to watch that wound heal. It healed from the inside out, closing from bottom to top all by itself. Before long, you couldn't even tell where she had been hurt.

Next, later that very same year, Rosey walked into our yard with a decent-sized wound on her rump. It was about as big as a silver dollar. It looked like maybe she had been shot by a pellet gun – the wound was definitely larger than what a BB gun would have caused.

Again, we tried to doctor her, and again we could not get close enough with our medicine spray can. However, it turned out that she didn't need doctoring this time. The process took a few weeks, but the wound healed just fine.

Rosey nearly always had scratches or cuts on her somewhere. We often wondered if we would get to see her grow up to be an adult. However, we knew that even though we worried about her all the time, and even though we helped take care of her, in the end she was on her own. We had to let her live her life as she wanted.

Chapter 6

Friends, Foes, and Food

Deer have friends and they have enemies. Of course, their best friends are other deer, but they are friends to farm animals as well. Often, deer graze in pastures right along with horses, sheep, and goats, and they might all drink from the same watering hole.

A horse in a nearby pasture became friends with Rosey. Goats and cattle in another pasture befriended her, and she had rabbits, squirrels, and birds all over.

And of course, she had her human friends – all of us in the neighborhood.

Most farm animals eat and drink during the day and sleep at night, but deer seem to move according to the moon rather than the sun. Rosey often grazed in the middle of the night. In the full moonlight, she could see and move safely. This meant she often slept during the day, which is how we could watch as she chewed her cud and rested.

Because deer have such big, brown eyes, people think they can see exceptionally well. While this is true, they can hear and smell even better. That is why, when they eat and move around, they try to walk into the wind. With the wind blowing into their noses and ears, they can smell and hear things a long way off. They eat a little and then raise their heads, looking around but mostly smelling and listening.

Researchers believe deer are color blind. We never designed a color test for Rosey, but she acted the same no matter what color clothes we wore. By acting the same, I mean she smelled every inch of them.

Because deer are color blind, hunters can wear yellow, red, orange, grey, or green. This helps hunters see each other, while the colors do not affect the deer.

You may not know that hunters are both enemies and friends of deer. Hunters kill deer, but they also help deer by reducing the population. Remember that deer do not roam more than about a mile from home, which means they eat and drink from their own territory. When the number of deer becomes too much for the territory to feed, many of them starve. Lack of food is one of the biggest threats to deer, and by reducing the population, hunters give the remaining deer more to eat.

Rosey's territory was not part of any hunting area. Still, the neighborhood could not help but worry about hunters.

In earlier days, from the late 1800s and before, the big enemies of the deer were mountain lions, wolves, coyotes, Native Americans, and cowboys. Deer as well as the cattle, buffalo, and other animals all over the United States supplied meat for humans and other animals for a long time.

Any way you look at it, deer have always been hunted.

Automobiles can also threaten deer, who cannot understand our road system. The trails they follow and the trails they make move around obstructions, while roads are mostly built straight through an area. Also, deer do not understand how to wait by the side of the road until a car passes, or how to look both ways before crossing. We often wondered if Rosey's mother had been hit by a car.

Grandpa and Rosey go for a walk

As for the threat of scarce food – well, as I have pointed out, Rosey enjoyed a great variety, so that never became a problem. She could choose from any plants she wanted and from lot of human food as well. Plus, she did not have to compete with other deer or any other animals. We might tend to think that a deer without sufficient food could simply go farther to find it, but remember, their territory is limited. There is no actual fence around it, but there might as well be.

As I mentioned, sometimes we objected to parts of Rosey's wonderfully varied diet. She quickly learned how to get at some plants by pushing over small fences with her head. One time, she got into special plants we grew in a pot. We hollered at her when she began eating them, and that nosy little deer knew exactly what we meant. Did she obey? Of course not. She just waited until we went inside, and then she would eat them.

After that came the bluebonnet incident.

Bluebonnets grew all over the area, and one time we dug some up, placed them in containers about as big as coffee cups, and set them along a neat row in a larger tray. We put the tray on the ground to water them with the hose.

Of course, nosy Rosey came to inspect. She smelled the little plants, which were not new to her at all. Oddly, though, while blue-bonnet plants stood in the ground right next to the tray, Rosey ate a plant out of the tray.

She leaned over, pulled one up with her teeth, and gobbled it down. This really surprised us, because we knew that she did not like bluebonnets. She always spit them out. They are slightly poisonous and probably do not taste good. Cows and other animals will not eat them, which is why the plants grow so well in an overgrazed pasture. Somehow, Rosey must have known that eating one little plant would not make her sick.

Suddenly, in a matter of just seconds, Rosey started pulling all of the bluebonnets from the tray and spitting them out.

We never quite figured out why. She liked eating the flowers everyone in the neighborhood planted, so was she showing us her dietary preferences? Was she warning us that they were poisonous?

Or was she just being mischievous?

Chapter 7

The "Teenage" Years

The seasons came and went, and Rosey grew older right along with the rest of us. No longer a baby or a "toddler," she made her presence felt in many ways throughout our community. Besides continuing to use the neighborhood as her personal cafeteria, she also more clearly outlined her territory. She even liked to roughhouse.

I remember that one day she acted especially spunky. She pranced around, jumping up and down, doing a little deer dance and obviously feeling happy. She wanted to play. Deer often playfully bump heads with each other, and poor Rosey had no one to join in any deer games.

I noticed an aluminum lawn chair nearby, and on an impulse, I snatched it up and held it in front of me, like a lion tamer at a circus. I pushed it toward Rosey. She jumped to the side. I pushed again, and she jumped to the other side. Then she rushed toward me, slapping at the chair with her front feet. I could tell she was only play fighting, because her ears stood straight up. Any time she prepared to fight seriously, she laid her ears straight back against her neck.

In her imagination, that chair was another deer. We wrestled and wrestled.

Female deer can use their front legs and hooves as weapons. The hooves are sharp enough to cut. The females are not aggressive and do not fight much, but they will protect themselves and their young. They will paw the ground and swing those razor sharp hooves when they need to.

Besides playing with us whenever she could, Rosey also probably enjoyed many adventures in the woods. She created her own trails. The tunnels she completed through the dense brush and trees were her favorite ways of getting from one place to another. Rabbits, opossums, skunks, and other small animals helped wear down the grass along those trails, but Rosey's sharp hooves did most of the work. Just imagine what 20 or 30 deer would create. Because Rosey made the trails by herself, they were very difficult to spot.

White-tailed deer create trails somewhat similar to our own road systems. Usually, there is one main trail with others branching off from it. The paths wind through thick growth, over open pastures, and around large trees. All deer use them. Sometimes the trails change because food places or watering holes change. Every trail is there for a purpose.

One time a dead tree fell over Rosey's trail. Although she could have easily jumped it, she preferred to go around. After that, her new, side path became a well-worn detour. Given the option, it seemed Rosey preferred to go around rather than over an obstacle.

It might be wise for people to do that sometimes as well.

Rosey joined all our family reunions

Deer hide often. They are nervous and easily excited. At the first sign of anything that even hints of danger, they stop what they are doing, stand still, listen, smell, and hide. If pushed further, they run, moving rapidly through their secret trails.

Not Rosey, though. She did enjoy a couple hours of "hideout" time each day, when she would blend into the background to rest. But because everyone liked her, she had little to fear.

Remarkably, not even gunfire scared her. Our grandchildren would come out and shoot their shotguns at clay pigeons, and Rosey would be right there, nosing around in the middle of it all. On July 4th, when we shot fireworks, she ignored them while harassing everybody for a handout of food.

Because she was not scared, and because her age resembled that of a teenager, she liked to do things that seemed to us like teasing. One day, for example, Grandpa was on his knees using snippers to trim some bushes close to the ground. He did not know Rosey was anywhere around.

Suddenly, he felt his hat fly off his head. Startled, he jumped up and turned around. There was Rosey, licking that hat and pushing it along the ground. Grandpa figured she was licking the salt from the sweat on it. He managed to get it back on his head without too much trouble.

I say Rosey was kind of like a teenager. Usually, it is difficult to determine the age of a deer. As part of our deer education, we learned that the number and condition of their teeth are good indicators (the same is true for sheep and goats). One problem with that, though, is that you cannot walk up to a deer and say, "Alright now, open wide please."

Fawns are born with eight front teeth on the lower jaw. Remember, deer have no front teeth on the upper jaw; instead they have a tough and rough gum or pad. When Rosey was about one month old, she had cut all of her premolars, which are smaller than the molars. In nine months, all the molars came through and Rosey had a full set of teeth. There is a cap on the third premolar, which deer lose at around seventeen to eighteen months of age. When the cap is gone, all teeth are full size.

The teeth keep growing until the deer are about two, and ultimately deer end up with 32 teeth. The chewing and grinding over the years wear the teeth shorter, and we can gauge the age of deer based on the amount of wear on the teeth. The method is not always accurate, but it is the best we have.

Rosey did not like us bothering her jaw, although she would let us look in her mouth if we were careful. She let us examine her closely enough to notice all these changes over time. Fortunately, with her, we always knew the exact age because we just counted the years since she showed up.

Rosey as a "teenager"

Rosey roamed her territory through the trails she developed over the years. She ate all the time, it seemed, and harassed all of us for more food at every chance she got. She liked to wrestle and tease.

If she had been a person instead of a deer, we would have had to start talking about getting her a driver's license and a car.

Chapter 8

Rosey Finds a Friend

By 1987, when Rosey had been around our place for three and a half years, she was old enough to have fawns.

About November of each year, as the leaves drop from the trees, rutting season begins for all deer. This is the time when the bucks start to look for certain does (females), and the does become interested in the bucks. In other words, it is the time when deer find their mates.

During this time, every 28 days, the does can become pregnant. The actual time that they can get pregnant is short – only a 24 to 30 hour period in all of those days. If no bucks show up, the doe must wait another 28 days. Fawns are born in April to mid-June, or about seven months later.

In the wild, the big, older bucks claim more than one doe and try to protect them by fighting other bucks. Each fall they have their new antlers, which have been polished on trees and brush. The horns are slick and strong. Typically, the stronger and more experienced buck wins the challenge for the does, and the younger bucks have to move on to other territory.

If Rosey were out with a herd, she could have been back in the bushes, watching the bucks fight. Knowing Rosey's nosiness, though, she probably would have been right in the middle of all the action.

The young yearling bucks also want a family, and so they often have to move to new ground, where there are no older bucks. Sometimes they take one or two does with them, but usually they go alone. While they look for new territory, the young females stay with the parent herd until the herd eats all the way to the outside of the established territory. Then they inch out a little further, still staying fairly close to home.

This means the young bucks break the herd's tradition of staying in its area. Some people estimate that they move up to four or five miles out. Sometimes those bucks find does and sometimes they do not.

We wondered: Were there other deer herds within four or five miles of Rosey?

We wondered about that a lot this particular year, because of the way Rosey acted and looked. We definitely thought she wanted a family. Apparently, she had grown tired of being the only deer on Redbird Road.

For one thing, her musk glands grew larger. These glands are located on the inside of the hind legs, near the hinge (or knee). They secrete a fluid that the female deer uses to mark her territory. They also let any interested buck know where a doe is located. Normally, the glands on Rosey were about as big and thick as an oblong silver dollar, but we noticed they had puffed up to between one half to three quarters of an inch.

Rosey certainly could have provided a wonderful home for a young buck. The first requirement is food and water. Deer need wooded areas with low branches or bushes, which means the food is within reach. They look for creek bottoms or drainage ditches, which usually have abundant trees and bushes. Rosey's territory met all of those qualifications.

Does are usually about a year old when they have their first fawn, and it is a single birth. The next year they can have twins or triplets, if the range is good and there is plenty of food. During food shortages, they usually have only one. We estimated that Rosey's territory provided food sufficient for four fawns.

When a female has a fawn, the first thing she does is give it a bath, by licking it with her tongue. The tongue is so strong that the fawn is moved around. This back and forth action teaches the baby how to use its feet and legs.

Next, the does move their babies to another spot. In less than an hour after being born, new fawns can wobble along beside their mothers. The mothers nurse the babies and then hide them. A mother tells its baby to lie down and wait until mom returns. Mom leaves and grazes. She always does this downwind from the fawn, in order to hear or smell anything important that might happen. The fawn itself has no smell of its own yet, except to its mother, so at this point no wild animals would come looking for it. A little fawn lying in a secluded place may look abandoned, but unless something out of the ordinary happened, the mother is nearby, observing.

Newborn fawns do not fear people, and if you found one you could easily pick it up. You should not do this though. People have their own smell and they will leave that odor on the fawn. Sometimes, that can be enough to prevent the mother from returning. Humans should always leave the little fawns alone with the other deer.

As you might tell from my description, observing all this is amazing, and everyone on Redbird Road would have been so happy if Rosey could have had a little fawn of her own. After all, here she was with plenty of food and water, plus a lot of other care from humans, but no other deer to share her paradise. She would not leave Redbird Road, because it was her territory, but surely she wanted the companionship of a buck.

Me and Rosey

One day, a neighbor who was outside building a fence, spotted a deer near some bushes. Just seconds earlier, nosy Rosey had been right there beside him watching the construction, so he knew it was not her. This other deer stood about 300 yards away. It had horns, and it seemed very cautious.

Then our neighbor spotted Rosey, who, it was obvious, had also seen the other deer. She looked, she sniffed, and she listened, her ears shifting back and forth.

In the distance, the buck stood pawing the ground a little, swinging his head down low and moving it up high. He snorted. He smelled, looked, and listened. Rosey started over to him and he watched. Then she started running, and so did he – except in the other direction. Rosey kept after him until he jumped an old fence.

Of all things, she had chased him away. Maybe she didn't want a companion after all. Maybe she was just particular.

However, about two weeks later, another neighbor said he spotted a buck. Apparently, Rosey's visitor had not given up so easily.

For a few days, Grandpa and I stopped seeing Rosey at all. Squirrels and rabbits ate the corn we set out for her. We thought maybe she preferred whatever the neighbors fed her, but they all said they had not seen her either. They thought she was at our house.

Soon, everyone started checking. The neighbors with five dogs said they had not seen her. The neighbors with the goats said she was there two days before but not since. Even the retired neighbor who stayed home most of the time had not seen her.

Once again, the whole neighborhood felt disturbed.

A few days later we talked to a neighbor who lived at the end of the road, kind of secluded from the rest of us. On Saturdays, he went to the local grocery store and often visited with the residents of Redbird Road on his way home. We realized no one had asked him about Rosey. When we did, on that first Saturday after she had gone missing, he said, "Yes, I have seen them."

Them?

Yes. Them. He had seen two deer walking side by side.

Later that same day, we saw Rosey again. Or Marcie. Or Deerie. Or Bambi. Or whatever each household called her. Everyone was so relieved to have her back, looking well and unharmed. She was "ours" again.

She had an adventure none of us could share with her. She had done what she wanted to do. She had everything in her territory that was required for a yearling buck: plenty of food and water, no other bucks to fight, and her own good company.

Would Redbird Road have a deer family?

Chapter 9

Rosey – and Sometimes I – Raise a Family

A year later, in late November, I opened the front door of our cabin and gasped at what I saw: a magnificent, giant, eight-point buck deer, standing only 50 feet away.

I held my breath, inched back inside, and stammered to Grandpa, "Th...There's...There's a huge buck outside."

Grandpa jumped up, came over, and quietly opened the door. The deer was still there. As we admired it, Rosey let out a loud snort and dashed away. Maybe she was scared of him, because it sure was a big deer. The buck ignored us and took off after her.

Even though a year had gone by since we first saw that one young buck in the area, Rosey had not given birth to any fawn. Then, on this

November morning, I had spotted her pushing up against the cabin, standing as close to it as she could possibly get. Something seemed wrong, and that was why I opened the front door.

During the next few days, we saw the two of them hanging around together. Apparently she overcame her fear. Next thing we knew, just as quickly as he appeared, he disappeared. We all wondered where he came from, and if he was the same buck Rosey had met last year. Of course we had to name him, so we called him "Chuck." Chuck the Buck.

"Chuck" the buck

We watched Rosey closely, and sure enough, she started getting fatter. By June of that year – 1990 – we could tell it was getting close, and then one morning she walked up and her belly was flat. Excitement spread all over the neighborhood.

When a week had passed, a neighbor and I decided to follow Rosey. We desperately wanted to see that new baby. All morning long, Rosey would just munch on brush and leaves and look at us as if to say, "Why are you following me?" We went through heavy brush, briars, and weeds, and all we got was scratched up and wore out.

We knew that even though Rosey was tame, her natural instincts were to hide a baby, even from us. And although she herself had no mother to teach her how to be a deer, her instincts remained.

Finally, one day as we watched from a distance, we saw her tiny fawn! It had long, spindly little legs and would lie down without moving until Rosey called it. We were so excited that I designed announcements and sent them out to all the friends, relatives and neighbors who had met, fed, and petted Rosey over the last five years.

We named the fawn – a girl – "Rosebud." We even sent out birth announcements to friends and family.

At about two weeks old, the baby started following Rosey around. A week later, when our grandchildren Sara and Clay were visiting,

I called to them, "Here comes Rosey with her baby. Be quiet and it will come right up to us."

We enticed her with her favorite food – chips.

All of a sudden Sara yelled, "Look Mammaw, there's two of them!"

I said, "That's just a feed sack lying out there." I looked closer. "At least I think it is."

"No, Mammaw, there are two babies."

I looked again. "Well I'll be."

Two of Rosey's fawns

All this time we assumed she had had only one fawn because it was her first. Apparently, since Rosey was five years old, nature compensated. Also, since there were no other deer around and we lived in a thick forest of oak trees with lots of acorns, Rosey would have no problem feeding two.

We later discovered that she kept them separated so it would be harder for a predator to find them. At about three weeks, the fawns can keep up with the mother, and so after that they all stay together.

Now we had to come up with another name for another baby, so we named it "Thorn," since we thought it was a boy. The two little fawns ran, jumped, and played together and stayed right with their mother. Even though Rosey was not wild, they were, so we got to observe the life of two wild fawns as closely as is humanly possible, though of course we couldn't touch them. They learned to like the same foods and treats as their mother, and all together, it was just as much fun as observing Rosey for all those years.

"Chuck the Buck" showed up again that fall, and the next year Rosey had two more beautiful fawns. Her first two were still around, so this meant Rosey was developing her own herd. Each year Chuck came back and ran off the yearling bucks, which left to find their own territory. Hunters harvested some of those, but one always showed up to breed Rosey and the other does. By the third year, Rosey was an old hand at being a mother. She was re-populating our little area of Texas. Some of her babies started having babies of their own.

Over the next few years, Rosey kind of became the head mother in the area, what we might call a matriarch. For example, one day a neighbor called and said she had found a young fawn caught in a fence and covered with fire ants. She wondered if it belonged to Rosey, and so she brought it over to our place. Right away, Rosey starting licking it to clean it up. The little fawn started nursing from Rosey, so we guessed that yes, it might be hers. And later, we did see three fawns following her around. Was it hers all along, or did she adopt it?

Years later, a friend found a fawn on the side of the road. Its mother had been killed by a car. The woman brought it to me because she knew about my wildlife rescue class. I took the deer home and tended to it for a day or two.

One day Rosey walked up, so I took the baby outside to see what would happen. I set it down and wouldn't you know, Rosey walked right to it, licked it, and let it nurse. Luckily, her own two babies were about the same size. We knew for sure that this one was not hers. So right away, we knew that deer – or at least our deer Rosey – would adopt other deer and raise them as their own.

Another year a neighbor called me and said Rosey was over there, under the porch trying to have a baby, and apparently having trouble.

I left the cabin as quickly as I could, but by the time I got there, it was too late. The baby's head had turned backward, and it smothered and died. We coaxed Rosey out from under the porch and finished delivering the baby. We waited a while, and when she did not have another one, we hoped she had already delivered one earlier and that it was okay.

We were thrilled to find out our guess was correct. However, Rosey raised only one fawn that year.

Next year, we decided, we had better watch her closely.

Sure enough, one morning that very next spring, I was out watering my yard and here she came. She stayed a while, and I began to think she had started her labor. She started to walk off, but then an amazing thing happened: she stopped, looked at me, and made the noise that she used to call her fawns.

At first, I decided it was just a coincidence, but she kept doing it, looking back at me and calling. I yelled inside to Grandpa, "She's calling me. She wants me to follow her!"

His voice came back, doubtful. "She's what now?"

"She's calling me. She takes a few steps, stops, looks back at me, and bleats like when she's calling her fawns. Bring the camera and come on."

I followed her into the woods to a little clearing. She lay down and called me again. I could tell she was really in the middle of labor, and when I got close I could tell the same thing that happened last year was happening again. The tiny fawn's head was trying to turn backward. Its little feet, only about the size of my fingers, were sticking out.

There was only one thing for me to do, so I did it. I grabbed those tiny feet, put my thumb on the baby's nose, waited for a contraction, and gently pulled out a fawn.

Rosey stood, licked the fawn all over, and lay back down. The baby got up on its wobbly little legs and walked over to me. Maybe she thought I was its mama!

A few minutes later, Rosey approached me, licked my hands, and then licked the fawn again where I had touched it. She was trying to clean off all the smell so no predator could find her baby.

Rosey's twins right after I helped with their delivery

Soon, she started having contractions again. This baby came out fine by itself, but it was much smaller than the first. They were both males. I thought about taking one, raising it on my own, and having a fully tamed deer. But since they were both bucks, I decided against it. Bucks that have no fear of humans can be very dangerous, especially during the breeding season.

I had delivered two fawns! Grandpa got there with the camera and I took many pictures of those babies. Remarkably, Rosey never hid those two from us. That very first evening, she brought them up to the cabin, almost as if she were saying, "Your two grandkids are doing just fine."

Seeing as how I delivered baby deer, I suppose I should have known that before long I would be babysitting them.

That is exactly what happened.

In May, a few years later, as we left to head back town, we saw Rosey lying by the garden. We stopped, thinking that maybe she had new babies. And right there, we saw two brand new little does.

The next door neighbor, Darlene, and I decided to tame them by raising them right now, before they became scared of humans. We each brought one home. Unbelievably, every day, three times a day, Rosey would stop by Darlene's house; Darlene would take the baby outside and let it nurse. Next, Rosey would come to our place and nurse the other baby. She didn't mind a bit that we had them. She seemed to know she could trust us.

After a couple weeks, when the fawns grew big enough to follow her, we gave them back to Rosey. As soon as they left with her, they were almost wild again. This proved to us that, to truly imprint them on humans, deer have to be bottle-fed. Those two little ones, who we named "Mia" and "Maya," would come closer to us than the other ones, but they definitely stayed wild.

One of Rosey's offspring at the clearing where I helped
deliver the baby

Chapter 10

Strong to the End

Rosey seemed prone to accidents. Maybe it was just because we all knew her and watched her so closely, but it sure seemed she always found a way to hurt herself. Despite this, she recovered from one injury after another, well into her old age.

One year she jumped a barbed wire fence and tore off part of her udder. A flap as big as a person's hand hung down from her. We could not take care of this injury ourselves, and so all the neighbors pitched in to pay for a veterinarian.

The vet said he could cut the tear off and stitch the area, but he did not know how much medicine to give a wild animal to make her sleepy enough for the procedure. If he made her fall asleep completely, she might not wake up. He decided to give her more sedative than he would a dog but less than he would a horse.

He sedated her, laid her down, and tied her so he could do the work. He cut off the flap and sewed the tear, which removed one of her nipples. I played the role of nurse, helping hold down one of her legs.

However, the vet did not use quite enough sedative, because suddenly Rosey started kicking. The vet yelled toward me, "Let go of her leg! Get back!"

I followed those orders as fast as I could. He continued, "She's as strong as a horse in those legs. If she wanted to get up now, a pickup truck couldn't hold her back. Be sure and stay where she can't kick you."

We got back into position and finished the operation. When we backed off, Rosey stood and staggered around, her tongue hanging out of the side of her mouth. But a few minutes later she had recuperated enough to go find her babies.

We worried that the procedure would make her milk dry up, but it didn't, and she continued to nurse two babies using three nipples – that year and for the rest of her life.

The two babies I delivered

I already mentioned the time she was attacked by the pack of dogs, or perhaps coyotes. That's when most of the meat got torn off her leg, and when Grandpa and I tossed the watered-down iodine on her whenever she got close to us. She caught on to that very quickly, and would get close to us only if that bottle were nowhere in sight. After that sore healed, from the inside out, we could never even spot a scar, even though the leg bothered her when she got older.

I also mentioned the time she got shot in the hip by a small gun, probably either a pellet gun or a .22. We gave her antibiotics, which she promptly spit out. So we had to start hiding them in the food we gave her. That wound healed from the inside out as well.

The worst injury was a gaping hole at the bottom of her chest. We figured she either had been shot or had staked herself on a sharp post. Luckily, the wound was low enough down that it could drain, but still, by the time we found her, a bad infection had already set in. She was swollen like a balloon, like her hide had pulled away from the meat. You could squeeze on her leg or anywhere else, and the hide just sank in and popped back out. When she walked, she went "squish, squish, squish."

Her lung fluid was draining from the hole in her chest. Needless to say, the whole situation was awful, and also life-threatening.

We knew she needed antibiotic shots. We called the vet again, who gave us the medicine and said to give her shots twice a day.

Easier said than done.

The first shot went fine, but just as she did with the pills, Rosey caught on fast. From then on, the procedure required four men. One would hold her head while another would grab her back legs and throw her down. The third would lie on top of her, and the fourth would give her the shot.

Then one of them would say, "Ready…now," and everyone would jump off at once, very quickly, so they wouldn't get kicked in the head when they let her loose. This routine went on for about a week.

However, one time, everybody let go before Grandpa said, "Now."

There was Rosey, lying on the ground, with Grandpa on top of her like a wrestler. Her legs began to kick. We began to panic. Grandpa sprang up off her as fast as he could, barely escaping injury.

He did lose his pipe, though. For some reason, he had continued to hold that pipe in his mouth while they all held Rosey down. Somehow, when he jumped off unhurt, the pipe got bit right in two. Rosey barely missed his nose. Maybe she was just sending another warning, like she did with that young boy who petted her the wrong way.

Or, who knows? Maybe she just wanted him to give up the habit of smoking that pipe.

Either way, that was a close call. Grandpa said, "I believe that's enough now. Either she'll live or she won't. But at least all of us will live."

Grandpa with the pipe Rosey shattered

Rosey did live. She lived for twelve more years, until she was 21, which is at least twice as long as most deer live in the wild.

She had twins every year.

As she got older, life began to take its toll on her. Her ear, which had gotten cut before we discovered her, drooped more and more. She became blind in one eye, and she developed severe arthritis in the leg where she had been attacked. Her hair quit shedding like it once did, and so we combed and groomed her. She often got ticks in the corners of her eyes, but she would let me pick them out with tweezers.

We knew she did not have long to live, and we feared coyotes or wolves would soon get her. But she was one smart deer, and the older and more frail she got, the more she stayed close to our homes.

Finally, one day she went out behind the barn, lay down, and died peacefully.

Rosey at the ripe old age of 21, not long before she died

Rosey the nosy deer showed up in the spring of 1984 and died in the spring of 2005. She had twins every year for the last 15 years of her life. Her babies had babies, and today Redbird Road is populated with beautiful white-tailed deer. They look so much like her that sometimes I forget she's gone.

I keep expecting one of them to walk over to me, looking for a bag of corn chips.

Chapter 11

Our Teacher, or the "Gospel According to Rosey"

From the first day we saw Rosey, we started learning. My wildlife rescue class, the encyclopedia, and our grandkids' curiosity all combined to give us an education about deer and their habitat that we may have never gotten if she had not come into our lives.

We received another type of education from Rosey as well. It didn't come from books, but rather from the way she acted. In the end, she taught us as many lessons as any good teacher.

Here are a few of them.

1. <u>Be present and be hospitable</u>.

When family or friends come home, always show up to greet them and make them feel welcome.

2. <u>Have fun, and do what you do with passion</u>.

Feeding herself and her many offspring kept Rosey busy, but she always found time to run, jump, swim, play, and romp – she always burst with enthusiasm. She showed us the value of having fun and of being fun for someone else.

3. <u>Let people give you attention</u>.

Sometimes I seem to think I need to take care of everybody else. Rosey showed us that it is okay to let someone else take care of you sometimes.

Hugs are especially good.

4. <u>Eat with enthusiasm, but not so much that you choke</u>!

Rosey loved to eat, but it took only one time of eating too much, too fast, for her to learn not to do it again.

5. <u>Always be willing to make new friends – and be willing to be in a picture</u>.

Rosey befriended everybody who was friendly to her, and we all benefitted. Thank God for all the pictures and memories.

6. <u>Try new things</u>.

Think of all the food Rosey would have never tasted if she had been unwilling to try something new. If she did try something and didn't like it – like the time she tasted the bluebonnets – well then, she just didn't eat it anymore. The greatest risk is this: never taking risks.

7. <u>Set boundaries</u>.

Let people know, firmly and yet kindly, when they have invaded your territory. Of course, I don't mean territory like the land, which was Rosey's territory. I mean personal territory. If someone does or says something that makes you uncomfortable, it is okay to say so.

When that young boy rubbed Rosey the wrong way, she sure made it clear that she didn't like it, but she did so without hurting anyone.

8. <u>Face your problems head on, and you will find the path of least resistance</u>.

Rosey never ignored the obstacles she encountered, just hoping they would go away. Instead, she dealt with them directly, but when she did, she usually found a way around them. This meant she did not try to force herself right through the middle of a problem.

9. <u>When you have a big problem, ask for help</u>.

Every time Rosey got hurt badly, she came to us. She was not too proud to admit she needed help.

10. <u>Never pretend to be something you are not, and be comfortable in your own skin</u>.

Rosey may have been a unique deer, but she never acted like anything other than a deer. She communicated with us as directly and honestly as she could, and she never showed the slightest embarrassment about what she said.

11. <u>Use your natural, God-given instincts, and never lose your curiosity</u>.

Rosey always looked before she leaped. She closely observed every new situation she encountered. When she considered something safe or desirable, she jumped in with all she had. Both the observing and the leaping were her natural instincts.

12. <u>Good things result from bad things. Whatever happens to you was meant to be.</u>

When she was a tiny doe, Rosey got caught in a fence and almost died. A few years later, a pack of dogs or coyotes mangled one of her legs. These were terrible things, and I wish they never happened.

However, if she had never been caught in that fence, Rosey never would have been rescued by our rancher neighbor. That means she never would have found her family on Redbird Road.

And if she had never gotten that leg mangled, she would have never understood that we could nurse her back to health. That means she probably would have never asked for my help in delivering her baby that would have otherwise died.

I'm not saying that all those bad things were actually good. I'm saying that, if those bad things never happened, a whole lot of good things would have never happened either.

13. <u>Leave your story as a legacy.</u>

Her life became not only her story but also my story and "our" story.

14. <u>The greatest freedom is simply to live and to trust God in everything.</u>

ANNOUNCING

OUR NEWEST RESIDENT

NAME: Little Rosebud

DATE: June 21, 1989

WEIGHT: About 5 pounds

PARENTS: Rosie the Nosy Deer
and Chuck the Buck

ADOPTED GRANDPARENTS:
A. W. and Martha Tieken

SEX Unknown (We haven't been able to get close enough to tell, yet.)

The birth announcement I made for Rosey's first baby

A recent picture of one of Rosey's grandchildren

About the Author:

Martha Knight was born in Brownfield, Texas, about 40 miles southwest of Lubbock. The daughter of a Baptist minister, she moved to Georgetown in 1978, and she is a member of Crestview Baptist Church there. She was a real estate broker along with her appraiser husband – A. W. Tieken – at Tieken Appraisal Co., until he passed in 1995. Later she managed Vacation Getaways at Sun City Texas in Georgetown.

In 2001 she married Jesse Knight, who, like everyone else on Redbird Road, enjoyed a memorable and lasting friendship with Rosey.

Jesse Knight and Rosey

Today she owns and operates Martha's Treasure House, a gift shop in Walburg, Texas, where she sells her art and many handmade treasures.

Me holding one of Rosey's fawns

Rosey in her prime

With two of her babies

CPSIA information can be obtained
at www.ICGtesting.com
Printed in the USA
FFHW012141041218
49746754-54203FF